CM807999075

**A BOOK BY
BENJAMIN DRURY**

CULTURE

HOW TO RID YOUR ORGANISATION OF POLITICS AND CREATE MASSIVELY HIGH PERFORMING TEAMS.

THE CULTURE GUY

INSPIRE, MOTIVATE, CHALLENGE

Published by The Culture Guy (part of Cogiva Ltd.)
Sidcup. DA14 4QG.
www.thecultureguy.com

Publisher's Cataloguing-in-Publication data
Drury, Benjamin
      CULTURE: How to rid your organisation of politics and create massively high performing teams / Benjamin Drury
        p. cm.

ISBN-10: 1505816025
ISBN-13: 978-1505816020

acknowledgements **00**

come on in the water's great **01**

it's not just for yoghurt **11**

what's in it for me? **23**
+ stuff to do

what do you do all day? **41**
+ stuff to do

who's in, who's out? **85**
+ stuff to do

what's that you say? **111**
+ stuff to do

what happened in here? **127**
+ stuff to do

batter up! **155**

cultural truths **165**

about the one framework **171**

about the culture guy **177**

photograph acknowledgements **181**

Here's to the dreamers and the doers;

The thinkers and the actors;

The ones who see things

the way they should be, not the way they are!

The ones who act

and get things done, and change the world!

START HERE

COME ON IN THE
WATER'S GREAT!

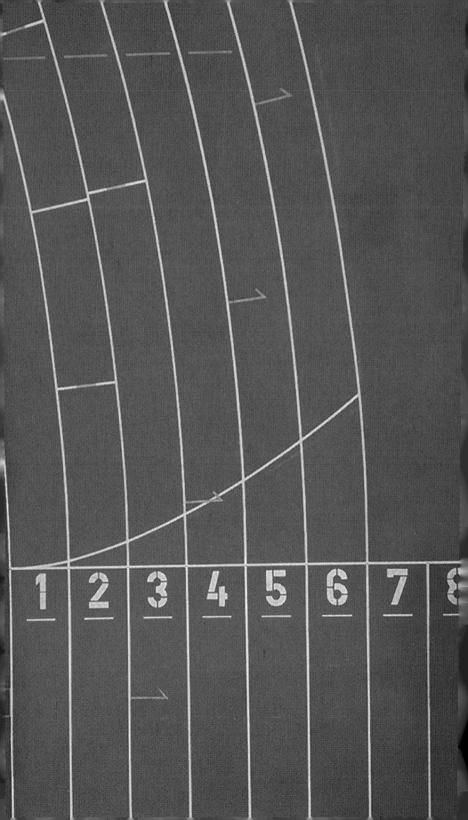

"What if there is no 'perfect moment'?
What if there is only right now?"

ANON

Imagine a world where every single person is fulfilled and passionate about their job. A world in which everyone loves getting up in the morning and going to work. A world where people really enjoy their jobs and work on projects that are meaningful to them in roles at which they are brilliant. Imagine every person coming home happy at the end of the working day feeling fulfilled, having worked on something of value to the world.

Imagine that! Imagine how different the world would be.

It sounds like an introductory synopsis from a dystopian novel where there is some secret underhanded power controlling people yet to be revealed later in the story as it unfolds.

But, what if it were actually possible? What if life were actually like this? How would the world change?

George and Richard Cadbury believed in this ideal way back at the end of the 19th Century, when they took over their father's chocolate business. At the time it was a small business in the heart of England, but it didn't remain small for long. George and Richard had other ideas and they set about crafting their grand vision. They not only improved worker conditions during a time when workers had very few rights, but they actually built an entire town in Bournville (UK) to ensure their workers had suitable accommodation and a safe, healthy place to live. They built sports clubs to allow their employees to remain fit and well and give them opportunities to socialise. They were groundbreaking with their employee benefits, giving employees a cash gift to start a pension in 1906. They supplied funding to provide some form of education for every employee under the age of eighteen, more than one hundred years before the compulsory school leaving age in England was raised to eighteen.

George Cadbury had a belief about the good that business could and should do.

"Nearly all my money is invested in businesses in which I believe I can truly say the first thought is the welfare of the workpeople employed."

GEORGE CADBURY

A more recent example is the Ritz-Carlton. Ritz-Carlton is a company that not only gives its employees responsibility but gives them the authority to do their job and properly empowers and equips them, allowing them to be brilliant. It is the only service company in America that has won the Malcolm Baldridge National Quality Award twice (a prestigious honour, awarded by the US Congress) and Training Magazine has called it the best company for employee training. Its motto (and mission) is simple: "We are ladies and gentlemen serving ladies and gentlemen." One of the amazing ways this is implemented is by permitting every single Ritz-Carlton staff member, without approval from their general manager, to spend up to $2,000 on satisfying a guest. And that's not per year. It's per stay. It's a meaningful amount that displays a deep trust in the staff's judgment.

Business in the 21st century gets a bad rap and sometimes rightly so. Capitalism, with its unchecked greed, leads to stories of workers being ignored, abused or worse, even killed in pursuit of profit for shareholders and billionaire founders and investors. The newspapers abound with articles on zero-hours contracts and drivers being paid less than minimum wage with no holiday or sick pay, due to some loopholes in employment law, whereby they are merely contractors and not employees at all. (Strange how if you get your income solely from one source you are considered employed for tax purposes, but not for legally required employee benefits.)

Think delivery drivers across the globe or food courier riders in London or read stories in the British press of companies, where people were fired for taking sick days and ambulances were regularly called to a warehouse after people collapsed on the job, fearing poverty if they took any time off.

It does not need to be this way. It shouldn't be this way. I believe it is possible to build a world where business takes the lead in creating a workplace for their employees to thrive. A place where people are understood and genuinely cared for by their employer. A place where people are more than happy to spend their time and effort in a worthwhile pursuit. And the amazing by-product of employees who love to work is that the organisation becomes more productive and improves their bottom line profits too.

The more businesses that choose to actively build this type of authentic culture, the closer we get to the imagined utopia. You reading this book is the beginning of that process.

I've spent over a decade studying successful companies. Investigating what makes companies like Ritz-Carlton or Cadbury different and the good news is there is a straightforward framework that anyone can follow. The less good news is that while it is simple to understand the framework, it is not easy to implement. That's why so few organisations actually manage to do it. It takes determination, commitment, hard work and perseverance, sometimes against vocal opposition. But, it is entirely possible to build a culture without politics and hidden agendas. A culture where teams are massively high performing and take so little management you won't know what to do with your time. It is absolutely possible to build a thriving culture that not only improves the lives of employees but also improves the profits of the business.

This book is the "how to" guide you need! It takes you through the four stages of The One Framework ™ - One Purpose; One Team; One Voice; One Focus - and helps you define and implement the ideal culture for your organisation - stopping to help you think through your particular organisation on the way.

But first, what exactly is culture?

IT'S NOT JUST
FOR YOGHURT!

"Culture eats strategy for breakfast!"

PETER DRUCKER

Imagine, one day you're walking through the town where you live, a route you walk on a regular basis. Suddenly a person coming towards you catches your eye. You recognise them, but can't quite place them. You've seen them before, but you can't remember where. You wrack your brains dragging up possible connections to figure out where you know them from, before they spot you and an embarrassing conversation ensues, while you try to recall their name. But you just can't remember them and it continues to nag at you: "Where have I seen them before?"

Then it hits you.

It's an old school friend. Someone you haven't seen for twenty years since you left high school at eighteen and went your separate ways. No wonder it took so long to dig up the memory!

After exchanging hellos and engaging in a brief chat, you realise that your lives have turned out very differently. The last twenty years have taken you to some very different places with very different experiences. You are settled and have a family. He is single, never married, with few friends around. He has just moved into town by himself and is starting a new job in a new place.

Your friend doesn't know many people in the town and from what you can recall he always seemed a reasonably sensible friend at school, so you invite him round for dinner the next evening in the hope of catching up, helping him out and perhaps rekindling a friendship.

As the next evening rolls around you prepare to welcome your guest. You frantically tidy the parts of the house that are in view. You carefully set the table: cutlery, crockery, wine glasses. You devise and craft a delicious menu: starter, main course and homemade dessert - orange chocolate mousse!

You ready yourself for some rich food, excellent wine and erudite conversation. Then your guest arrives - fifteen minutes late, but then isn't everyone? Pleasantries are exchanged, you introduce him to your wife and you all sit down to enjoy your evening. Then things get weird. Not good weird. Uncomfortable weird!

Your guest doesn't wait to be offered food or to be served, but instead starts grabbing food and filling his plate. Fast. And High! More than half the food is gone before you have a chance to pull in your chair. When was the last time he ate? Come to think of it, when was the last time he had human contact? Once satisfied he has "enough" food in front of him, he starts shovelling it in like a starved animal, barely breathing and only occasionally using a fork (the knife is never touched) seemingly unaware that other people are involved in this meal.

He is apparently in technology, although you hardly get the chance to ask him much. He has the 'gift of the gab' and doesn't stop talking for two whole hours, save to swallow the food that he hasn't already spat onto the table while speaking.

And it's not just the constant talking it's the language he uses! You find yourself hoping your children are asleep and can't overhear the monologue emanating from the dining room. Words never uttered in your house before. Some you've never even heard before!

The table manners; the language; the rudeness; the lack of common courtesy; the lack of social awareness. Who is this person? Was he like this all those years ago at school?

How are you feeling right now reading this story? Does it

make you feel tense? Annoyed? Frustrated? How would you be feeling if that was actually happening in your home?

It's quite uncomfortable, isn't it? I know the thought makes me feel extremely anxious. I would want it to be over as quickly as possible but I wouldn't know what to do if the situation really happened.

Should I be polite, finish dinner quickly, feign tiredness and usher him out of the house, remembering never to invite him again? Should I perhaps challenge him on the behaviour? What's the best and quickest way to end this nightmare? Ask him to behave more appropriately?

This is exactly what culture is! That little word 'appropriately'. The unwritten rules and values that you consider normal. The standard of behaviour that you would reasonably expect others to follow.

In my home and family we've created a culture. It may not be explicitly defined but it's there: standards of behaviour, expectations of how we speak and how we shouldn't speak, the etiquette of politeness, etc.. When those standards and expectations are violated, when someone cuts across my cultural expectations, it makes me extremely uncomfortable. Which is what happens when our hypothetical visitor comes to dinner. My culture has been disrupted and violated and it makes me uncomfortable.

DEFINING CULTURE

"Culture is a fuzzy set of basic assumptions and values, orientations to life, beliefs, policies, procedures and behavioural conventions that are shared by a group of people, and that influence (but do not determine) each member's behaviour and his/her interpretations of the 'meaning' of other people's behaviour."

H. SPENCER-OATEY

Culture is derived from the Latin word cultura which means to care for and grow. A culture is simply an environment where things grow. Good things can grow. Weeds can grow. What grows depends on the specific culture, but something will grow.

This concept of culture was first articulated by anthropologist Edward Tylor, one of the founding figures of social anthropology, in the late 19th century. He used the concept of culture to distinguish different actions and environments of groups on an evolving scale from 'savagery' to 'barbarism' to 'civilisation'. More recently, however, this concept was developed with a more inclusive thinking, defining culture free from any value judgment of which culture might be 'right' or 'better'. Who knows? Perhaps your hypothetical visitor has the more honest culture because there is no pretence. Don't we all want to be selfish really?

The idea we are building on in this book is the concept that culture simply exists and is the product of the shared values, behaviours and thoughts of a group. Any place where two or more people gather for a purpose a culture will exist. Either explicitly or unwritten there will be rules and expectations of how to behave. This is culture.

But why is culture important?

WHAT'S IN
IT FOR ME?

"If you are lucky enough to be someone's employer, then you have a moral obligation to make sure people do look forward to coming to work in the morning."

JOHN MACKEY, WHOLE FOODS MARKET

Wherever two or more people come together for a common purpose a shared culture will arise. Whether it's two people in a marriage, a few children in a group of friends at school or swathes of employees in a multinational corporation, when groups join up to achieve something they will generate and rally round a shared collection of behaviours, beliefs, values and expectations.

CULTURE TRUTH #1

*When people come together for a purpose
a shared culture will form.*

Think of your long lost school friend in the last chapter. When he came into your home you expected him to behave in a certain way. A way that shared your values. A way that stayed inside the boundaries of your opinion on what constituted common decency.

You had a culture in your mind that needed to be upheld, but when did you sit down and write out those expectations? At what point in your marriage or personal life did you discuss and articulate how you expected people to behave when they came into your house?

When did you compile your "Rules & Expectations" orientation pack?

My guess is you didn't. You may have discussed certain topics or expressed a few values in passing conversation, but I'm pretty sure you didn't specifically commit to paper the values and culture you wanted to build in your family.

(BTW: If you're part of a family and you haven't had this conversation in your family, then can I recommend Patrick Lencioni's book 'The Three Big Questions for a Frantic Family'.)

The thing is, it doesn't matter whether you spend time explicitly defining what you believe your culture should be or whether you allow it to develop organically unspoken over time, every single organisation, community or group of individuals, no matter how small or large, will develop a culture - a common set of social rules and values that influence and define everything within the organisation.

And if culture influences and affects every aspect of your organisation, then why would you leave it to chance? Why wouldn't you spend time crafting and implementing the exact culture you want to grow in your organisation? Why wouldn't you be clear and explicit about exactly how you wanted people to behave?

You wouldn't just go out and hire a random group of people to be your board of directors, would you?

How about we put an ad card in the local newsagents?

"Wanted - people with spare time to run a national corporation. No experience necessary. Travel costs provided. Position guaranteed to first ten applicants to apply."

That's just crackers! You'd be very careful with your selection process. You'd put candidates through a very stringent vetting process and a sequence of thorough interviews. You'd review past performance and gather recommendations from trusted advisors. You'd more than likely give them a lengthy probationary period with very clear expectations and desired outcomes before you hired them permanently. You'd put time, effort and money into making sure you didn't get it wrong. You can't afford to get it wrong. The future of your organisation depends on not getting it wrong.

Yet few organisations give the same level of attention to defining and developing their culture, even though the culture within your organisation will have a much more profound impact than the board of directors. (Although the board of directors would very much influence the culture, so they are not mutually exclusive! More on this in the chapter on people.)

CULTURE TRUTH #2

For better or worse, your culture will influence every aspect of your organisation.

Your culture will infect every member's behaviour AND every member's interpretation of others' behaviour and it will manifest itself at several different depths within an organisation: the space and the environment your organisation builds; values, beliefs and assumptions that people hold; the behaviours people display and their interpretation of other people's behaviour; employees interactions with clients; the amount of effort employees exert; the respect people show for leadership and peers; the clothes people wear; the external branding; the internal branding; the processes and procedures; people's phone manner; the quality of the equipment you use. The list is endless.

Everything is impacted by your culture.

Whether you like it or not, your organisation has a culture, and it will affect how every part of your organisation performs, so don't leave it to chance.

Consider, GivaSure Ltd., a (totally made up) multinational organisation selling insurance to car owners across Europe. It has grown rapidly over the last ten years selling its very cheap products online in 13 countries and now turns over several hundred million pounds sterling a year. It started off as a small startup, a disruptive alternative to the large insurance companies that were offering cheap loss leader products to new customers and then inflating prices for existing customer renewals.

The founders were fed up with this underhand tactic and so launched an alternative brand to give customers better deals across the board, providing fair and equitable pricing for both new and existing customers.

Because it was small and nimble and the founders were available to answer questions and develop new products the company thrived and was able to offer fair prices to all, exceptional customer service and some innovative pricing options for their car drivers. As the company grew, though, the founders became busier and less available. They had to be more focused on running the business than doing the work on the ground so they left that to their team. The founders, however, struggled to let go and didn't want decisions made without their opinion. They were concerned that their team wouldn't be able to deliver the 'brand' or understand the core business as well as they did. They'd built the company and, up until this point, they'd controlled every aspect of the business, which is what made it successful. They wanted to maintain that, so their input was necessary, and on all matters it was final. They ran a very tight ship, and over the years it became clear that they were not to be questioned. One's superiors are never contradicted and no one ever disagrees with management.

On the one occasion it did happen, a few years ago, the individual concerned was severely reprimanded both officially with a verbal warning and unofficially through social repercussion - she stopped being invited to important meetings and was left to do menial tasks that she couldn't get wrong.

The employees soon learned not to disagree with superiors.

Over time, the founders became less and less innovative in their thinking. They were busy running their growing company and protecting what they had built. They didn't have time to spend on innovation and as no one else was allowed the freedom to develop ideas, the product offering got stale and lost its attraction to customers.

The founders were also less available to support their customer service team so had to develop 'foolproof' scripts that were not to be deviated from in order to stop the call centre staff making mistakes. Freedom to solve problems diminished and customer service quality slipped.

People felt like they weren't allowed to think. They were given the responsibility, but not the authority, to do their job. People felt unappreciated so staff turnover went up. In order to compete the prices were cut and costs were slashed.

No more free tea and coffee. No more company barbecues.

Pay rises were few and far between, particularly as there was little room for people to show initiative and excel. Everything changed and customers started to notice the changes. Marketing had to work harder to get new customers. They started reminding customers of where they started from: great customer service, fairer deal for customers, more innovative products. But those times had long gone and customers no longer believed the rhetoric. GivaSure started to look like every other inauthentic insurance multi-national simply because they failed to be explicit about and properly clarify and integrate the culture they initially set out to build.

The culture was not deliberately articulated, written down and clear to all. It wasn't protected, so everything in the organisation suffered.

THE 2P FABLE

GivaSure Ltd started exhibiting a phenomenon that I'm safe in saying everyone has experience at some point. If you've ever dealt with a bank or a utility company or a phone company, you will most certainly have experienced it. It's a phenomenon that I call "The Practice/Preach Fable" or "The 2P Fable". It's quite common in large organisations with big marketing budgets.

The basis of The 2P Fable is that a company prominently and deliberately articulates a mission and values via their prolific branding and marketing output, expressing something laudable and wonderful about their organisation and why doing business with them is uplifting and fulfilling and good for the world in general. However, when a customer eventually does come to interact with them, the verbally espoused culture bears no resemblance to the way the organisation operates in reality or behaves towards people. People are rude and the staff are unhelpful. The company shows little concern for customers and it is in no way uplifting!

It's just empty marketing rhetoric. An unfulfilled promise. A marketing construction with no basis. It's not real. It might have been once upon a time, but right now, it's just not true. What perhaps once was, has not been protected. The culture has been left to develop organically and reached a destination that isn't where the founders want it to be.

The fact is that words are not enough. A culture is built and grows out of what people do, the way they behave, the actions that are praised or punished and not by what is merely spoken.

Spend time defining your culture and designing every part of your organisation to deliver the behaviour and attitudes that you want from your people. If you leave it to chance, you will end up somewhere you don't want to be!

The remainder of this book will help you start to define, articulate and implement the culture you want in your organisation.

Defining and implementing a new culture will not be a quick process. In fact, if your organisation is large and has been around for a while, this process could take several years. This book will start you on that journey and if you're committed, you will begin to reap the benefits in small ways very quickly.

So how do you go about building a culture? First you must define your purpose...

There's some space overleaf for you to do some thinking...

(You can use this page too if you like)

Your ideas
go here

Think about an organisation that you wouldn't want to be part of. Why not? What about it makes it unpleasant? Think about the sort of organisation you want to be part of. How does it feel to work there? What's the atmosphere like? How do people behave towards one another? What does the office look like? How do the leaders communicate?

Put your thoughts down here. Add notes, lists, doodles, drawings etc to help you describe it.

WHAT DO YOU
DO ALL DAY?

"We believe that every organisation has a North Star – a guiding purpose that remains true over time. Often the trick is finding that North Star through the haze."

KEITH YAMASHITA & SANDRA SPATARO

An organisational purpose is your north star! It's your guiding light. It explains why your people come to work and defines what they do all day. Your purpose is what pilots your organisation into the future and against which everything your organisation does should be measured.

A purpose gives your team clarity, direction and focus and should be the very heartbeat of your organisation. The starting point for any business should be to ensure that you can clearly define your organisation's purpose in three parts:

The mission: what an organisation does. This is what happens each and every day at the coalface (Google "organises the world's information"; Disney "makes people happy").

The values: how an organisation behaves. This defines what is and is not appropriate to do while executing the mission. (For example Zappos aims to - "Be Adventurous, Creative, and Open-Minded; Build a Positive Team and Family Spirit; Be Passionate and Determined; Be humble".)

The vision: where the organisation is going. The business' vision should be "a big hairy audacious goal" that the organisation aims to achieve. (Amazon Kindle wants to make "Every book ever printed in every language all available in 60 seconds from anywhere on the planet").

We'll start with the mission.

According to dictionary.com a mission statement "sets out the purpose and work of an organisation." Simply put, an organisation's mission is what it does. For what purpose do employees start work each and every day? What is it that draws people into the office? When boiled down to a single sentence, what is it that you actually do day in, day out?

It's not the practical tasks you accomplish, but the outcome of those tasks that describes your mission. It's the answer to the question, what does your work achieve? Take this abridged conversation with a web design agency as an example:

What do you do?

Build websites and apps?"

But why?

Because people need good online tools and information

Why?

Because their customers are online

There are plenty of people out there building websites etc, why do you need to do it? What would happen if you weren't available?

Few business people understand the web and what it should cost, so they'd end up with inferior products and get ripped off too.

Why is that a problem to you?

Because I hate seeing people get ripped off and bad agencies taking advantage of hard working business people, so I want to put that right!

The mission of this company is to support small businesses to make good decisions and get value for money in technical development. They do not have a mission to build websites or mobile apps. Yes, that is what they do, but it's not their raison d'etre. It's not the purpose for which they exist. They are all about helping other people in that space.

Here are some other great examples from companies you will know:

Facebook "makes the world more open and connected."

Google "organises the world's information."

Disney "makes people happy."

Ford "provides personal mobility for people around the world."

Walmart "saves people money so that they can live a better life."

Your mission is the reason you exist, articulated as the outcome that occurs because you do what you do. To put it another way – what's the problem you solve and why?   Why do you exist? Or to look at still another way, what would need to happen for you to be no longer needed by your clients/customers?

The best way to get to the real heart of the what you do is to keep asking supplementary 'why' type questions until you can't ask any more questions. Somewhere in this process, you'll find the purpose for your existence.

Every organisation has a reason why they gather people to a place of work and pay them to do something. Even if you've not thought about it. Even if you've never articulated it or written it down. Even if you've never mentioned it to your workforce, your organisation has a mission. An organisation at its basic level is nothing more than "a relationship with a purpose" and therefore, simply a group of people that come together to execute a mission. Keith Yamashita and Sandra Spataro, best-selling authors of Unstuck, suggest that there is always a 'North Star' which guides an organisation.

Whether purposefully defined or organic and unspoken, your teams will be executing some version of an organisational mission. However, to rid your organisation of politics and hidden agendas, to get your teams working well together and increase productivity, you need to actively and consciously build and motivate great teams. That requires people to engage willingly in a common identity, a common understanding and purpose. Teams need to rally around a compelling purpose to become a great team, so you need to articulate your mission in a way that engages with the whole organisation.

So what's your mission? What does your organisation do? Can you articulate it in a single, simple sentence?

Here are a few helpful tips to help you start (and there are some exercises in the next few pages too!):

Make it inspiring. It needs to appeal to people's emotions. It needs to excite and motivate your teams. It should attract people to it like a moth to a flame.

Make it short. It needs to be memorable. More than two sentences and it's too complicated. People won't remember it.

Make it present tense. If you can't articulate it as if it's happening now, then it's not what you do, but instead, forms part of your vision. *(More on vision shortly.)*

Let's take a look at an example of a good mission statement. Here's the mission that Steve Jobs created for Apple in the 1980s when he began working on the Macintosh.

"Make a contribution to the world by making tools for the mind that advance humankind."

Now that's a great mission statement. It's present tense and describes what they do each and every day. It's emotive and inspires people to want to be part of it. It's a single sentence and easy to remember after just a few readings. It also contains a very clear why - to advance humankind. Apple is working towards the greater good.

As mission statements go this is pretty impressive and something I would be excited about getting up in the morning and going to work on.

Compare it to what's on the Apple website at the moment.

> "Apple designs Macs, the best personal computers in the world, along with OS X, iLife, iWork and professional software. Apple leads the digital music revolution with its iPods and iTunes online store. Apple has reinvented the mobile phone with its revolutionary iPhone and App Store, and is defining the future of mobile media and computing devices with iPad."

That's not a mission statement. It's just a list of products that they've already built. Nothing earth shattering revolutionary and definitely not inspiring. While all those products are cool, they're not really that mind blowing anymore. I'm not really inspired to be part of that organisation!

There is an oft-told apocryphal story that perfectly illustrates the importance of connecting people to a larger mission and fully engaging your team in understanding why they're doing what they're doing.

A man was walking through London one day when he came across a large building site with many tradesmen hard at work going about their business with varying levels of enthusiasm and interest. As he passed by, he caught site of three masons who were all working, chipping away at large blocks of granite forming them into bricks.

The first mason seemed unhappy with his job, frequently looking at his pocket watch and huffing and puffing as he carried on his work. When the man asked what it was that he was doing, the mason responded, rather curtly, "I'm hammering this stupid rock, and I can't wait 'til 5 when I can go home. I am so bored!"

A second mason, marginally more interested in his work, was hammering diligently at the granite. When asked what it was that he was doing, he answered, "Well, I'm moulding this block of rock so that it can be used with others to construct a wall. I'll sure be glad when it's done."

A third mason nearby was fervently hammering away at his block of granite, totally focused on his task. Now and then he would take the time to stand back and check his work, admiring what he'd accomplished. He chipped off small pieces until he was satisfied that it was the very best he could do, then moved onto the next rock. When questioned about his work like the other two masons before him, he stopped, gazed skyward and proudly proclaimed, "We're building a cathedral!"

Three different people. The same task. Three very different outlooks. Therefore, they approached their task very differently and no doubt produced a very different quality of workmanship.

The stone masons' different attitude to their work demonstrates the value of a clearly defined and engaging mission. The first mason merely broke rocks. He wasn't connected to the mission and didn't appreciate why he was doing it. He was disheartened and lacked motivation. In contrast, the third stone mason in our story clearly grasped the bigger picture - the what and the why of the mission: "creating amazing buildings" - and he went about it with enthusiasm and purpose. His work had meaning. He used his skills to take part in building amazing edifices. He had a mission!

A WORD OF CAUTION

Before we move onto values, a word of caution about your mission statement. Your mission should not be about making money. Making money is not your mission as a business. Let me repeat that for emphasis (and dramatic effect). Making money is NOT your mission as a business.

Don't get me wrong. Organisations need money. Without money, a business will not survive, but it is important to differentiate between purpose and necessity. For example, in order to live, humans must breathe, but breathing is not the purpose of life. So too with businesses. They need money to survive, thrive and grow. Money, however, like oxygen, while a necessity, is definitely not a good reason for existing. It's merely a tool to help achieve your mission. So make your mission about more than just money.

George Merck II, the former head of a global pharmaceutical firm Merck, expressed this notion very well in a speech he made to the Medical College of Virginia in 1950:

"We try to remember that medicine is for the patient. We try never to forget that medicine is for the people. It is not for the profits. The profits follow, and if we have remembered that they have never failed to appear. The better we have remembered it, the larger they have been."

GEORGE MERCK II

If you want to inspire people to build a great organisation focus on the heartbeat of the organisation and not the balance sheet and you'll build something of financial value as well.

More thinking time questions
on the next two pages...

(Dont forget to use this space too...
.....we love trees!)

Thoughts &
ideas

What does your organisation actually do? What does it produce? What's the service or product? Now ask why. Continue to ask why until you uncover the reason that you do what you do? Think about the problem you solve for your clients and the reason you get excited about the solution!

So you have your inspiring, simple mission statement and now everyone in the organisation knows why they do what they do. But are there any rules about how we should do it? Can we just do whatever is necessary to execute our mission? Are there any lines we shouldn't cross in pursuing our mission?

There are always rules. There is always an agreed way of doing things. Like the unwritten rules our vulgar dinner guest contravened in the opening chapter, where people come together for a purpose there are rules we call values that everyone is expected to follow or face some kind of sanction.

The second part of your organisational purpose is your values.

An organisation's core values are the operating principles that guide internal conduct and relationships with customers, partners, and shareholders. Core values define how a company and its people will (or at least should) behave.

For example, Johnson & Johnson say that their "first

responsibility is to the doctors, nurses and patients", a value which was put to the test when a voluntary product recall cost the company $100 million.

Or consider Volvo whose core value is safety. They haven't always produced the best looking cars on the market, but have consistently been on top of the safety rankings. They even used this lack of style in some of their early commercials that declared "they're boxy!"

The key thing to realise about values is that they describe how an organisation behaves; not how it wants to or should behave but how the organisation actually behaves. If Johnson & Johnson had not recalled their product, then their first responsibility would not be to patients and doctors, regardless of what their corporate PR team said! If Volvo didn't consistently prove to be safe in accidents, then safety is not a core value, no matter what they choose to tell customers in marketing literature.

(Side Note: After the emissions scandal in 2015 Volvo's core value of safety has rightly been seriously questioned.)

Patrick Lencioni, best-selling author, speaker and management consultant, says there are a number of different types of values to consider and organisations should be careful not to get muddled between these types of values. You need to understand the clear distinction between core values, permission-to-play values and aspirational values to effectively define your organisation's purpose. The values you should include in your purpose should be your core values. Those values that truly describe how you actually behave. Anything else would be inauthentic (but we'll talk more about that later in the chapter on voice).

Permission-to-play values are the ground floor standard by which everybody is required to abide to be a part of an organisation. They are simply the minimum standard of behaviour expected from an organisation to do business and they are often seen in poorly thought through mission statements in organisations that really have no values! Character traits like integrity, honesty, respectfulness, great communication, etc. usually provide a smokescreen for an organisation that has no clearly defined purpose. These are simply permission to play values. Values that if you didn't operate within for the majority of the time, people would stop doing business with you.

These values should provide a platform on which all must build and do not actually distinguish one organisation from its competition. We're not referring to these values, they should just be there like desks and phones - present in all organisations without question.

Aspirational values are those which an organisation would like to display, but don't. They describe how an organisation feels they should behave, but not necessarily do at the present time. These are the values that maybe need some work and effort to implement across an organisational culture. They don't come naturally and perhaps will form part of your vision for the future of the organisation. We are not dealing with these values either. Add them to your strategy, but not your purpose.

In this chapter, we are discussing only core values.

Core values are the behaviours which a company would go out of business to protect. The ones you would not compromise on even if it meant the end of your organisation. These are the behaviours that differentiate you from your competitors. These values are foundational to the organisation. They are absolutely non-negotiable, immutable and demonstrated day in, day out throughout the organisation. They are values that customers would use as adjectives if they tried to describe your organisation. They are clear to everyone both inside and out of the organisation, even if they are elusively difficult to articulate succinctly or have yet to be overtly defined.

To illustrate the point of core values, take this story that Herb Kelleher, former CEO of Southwest Airlines told after receiving a letter from a disgruntled customer when one of his flight attendants used humour during the pre-flight safety briefing:

> "In the event of a landing on water, we will bring round fresh towels and cocktails!"

When asked about the company's response, Herb Kelleher said, "most companies would have apologised to the customer, given her some form of gift or compensation and chastised the flight team for their poor and inappropriate behaviour. I didn't – I sent a short, three-word response to the lady. It said simply, 'We'll miss you!'"

One of Southwest Airlines core values was fun, and it was so central to their organisation that if customers don't like it, they would be better off choosing a different airline. Herb Kelleher wasn't prepared to compromise his core values. He'd rather lose a customer.

This section is concerned with helping you to define what your core values are. The values which are resolutely and uncompromisingly held even in the face of serious consequences, even at the risk of losing complaining customers.

To ascertain your company's core value, you simply need to ask yourself one question:

Is there anything you wouldn't do in pursuit of your mission?

Before we get into that though, we started this chapter with a question that I am often asked: "Why do organisations need to bother with defining their core values? Surely an organisation should be able to employ whatever tactics necessary, within legal parameters, of course, to achieve its mission?"

It's a fair question and on the surface seems correct.

However, although this hypothesis seems to present a sensible plan of action, research suggests the opposite to be true. Having no clear value structure can actually be detrimental to any organisation's long-term success.

Francis Fukuyama in 'Trust: The Social Virtues and the Creation of Prosperity', shows that communities operating from a common value base can prosper even in the adverse circumstances of a poor economy and create wealth out of very little indeed.

Peter Berger, University Professor of Sociology at Boston University, says that even a free economy requires trust and shared values to operate well.

In business, there are a lot of factors which are outside of your control and the landscape changes often and swiftly. Jim Collins asserts in Good to Great that the key to building a successful organisation is to hold a very clear understanding of immutable core values and preserve these at all costs. Any changes to the rest of the organisation can be made in line with the ever-changing requirements of the market without impinging on its core principles.

"Preserve the core and stimulate progress."

If you want to be a robust organisation that thrives even when times are tough, you must build on a set of agreed principles. You hold a set of immutable core values that remain unchanged regardless of the ever moving sands of strategy, finance and market forces.

The story of J. Urwin Miller is another wonderful illustration of core values in action.

In 1934 Miller become the General Manager of the Cummins Engine Company, which was founded by his great-uncle, to design, build and service power technologies. Over 80 years later, it is a Fortune 500 company operating in 160 countries across the world, with nearly $10 billion in turnover.

Miller, a committed Christian, was motivated to approach business as a form of discipleship, acting with integrity and honesty. In the 1930s, Miller supported the formation of a union at his organisation, Cummins, which was contrary to popular business practice at the time and long before he was asked. Later, in the 1970s Miller acted with integrity when he chose to shut down operations in South Africa in reaction to the government's ruling which would not allow a racially integrated workforce. Miller even encouraged the company to extend benefits to domestic partners of employees, at vast expense to the company, when no one else expected it.

Behaving so altruistically probably incurred a great

personal cost for Miller and it certainly cost Cummins Engine Company, but it was also non-negotiable: a core value on which he would not compromise.

To find your core values, ask yourself the same question that Miller asked himself: "What are the things that you will not compromise on in the pursuit of your mission?"

What are the three things that other people outside your organisation always say about you? What are the things that define you as an organisation compared with your competitors? It's these qualities that are your core values. It essentially defines how your people will behave in executing the mission.

Keep your core values to three or four and make them a single short sentence each. Just like the mission statement – short, easy to remember and in the present tense.

For example, The Culture Guy's core values are:

Lots of laughter - Work with passion, enthusiasm & commitment. Have fun and don't take yourself too seriously!

Make a better world - solve problems. Help people build a better place to live.

Do things well - be brilliant, makes things better, take risks and learn from good mistakes.

Everyone makes tea - we have no hierarchy, just roles and responsibilities. No one is too important to make and serve tea.

These are things at the heart of what The Culture Guy does, and we will not compromise on them – if we stop having fun then we will stop doing business. From CEO to secretary we won't hire people who are too important to make tea for their team. We are really clear about what we will and will not do in pursuit of the mission. These are the values that we would go out of business before we compromised.

CULTURE TRUTH #3

A culture is only truly defined by the way people behave and not what people say!

If you want to rid your organisation of politics and hidden agendas, you need to be clear about what you will and will not do in pursuit of your mission and everyone needs to be behind it.

We'll leave the final word on values to Herb Kelleher again:

"Having a simple set of values for a company was also a very efficient and expedient way to go, because if somebody makes a proposal and it infringes on those values, you don't study it for two years. You just say, 'No, we don't do that.' And you move on quickly."

HERB KELLEHER

How will you
behave?

What are the behaviours that people get into trouble at your organisation for NOT doing? What are the things that people get disciplined for doing? How would your customers describe your organisation?   Great service? High quality product? Always fun to work with? What behaviours would you go out of business to protect?

You now know what you do and how you want to do it. The final part of the purpose puzzle is: Where do you want to go?

Or to put it in business language: "What's your vision?"

The definition of vision is 'the act or power of anticipating that which will come to be; a vivid, imaginative conception or anticipation.' A vision is a picture of what your organisation will be or do in future.

For example, Amazon Kindle wants to make "Every book ever printed in every language all available in 60 seconds from anywhere on the planet." Nike aims "to bring inspiration and innovation to every athlete in the world."

Your vision is simply an exciting and challenging view of your organisation's future.

According to the author and management speaker Jim Collins', one of the key things he encourages organisation to do is create what he calls a "BHAG" or "A Big Hairy Audacious Goal." (His term for vision.)

A BHAG is a vision that falls into the grey area of what might be possible and what seems impossible. It doesn't just inspire people, it challenges them to be more than they ever believed possible. It seems impossible, but might just be doable if everything comes together. It's on the boundary of what's believable but excites people with what might be. It draws them in to be part of something incredible and exciting. A well-articulated vision grabs people on an emotional level, drawing them into being part of something bigger than themselves.

In his speech to Rice University in September 1962, President Kennedy set the ultimate BHAG saying, "We choose to go to the moon". What an enormous vision of the impossible that just might be doable.

"We choose to go to the moon in this decade and do the other things not because they are easy, but because they are hard, because that goal will serve to organize and measure the best of our energies and skills, because that challenge is one that we are willing to accept, one we are unwilling to postpone, and one which we intend to win."

JOHN F KENNEDY

Put a man on the moon! Go into space and put a person on another planet. (I know, technically the moon is a satellite!) Now that's a big hairy audacious goal if ever there was one. And they did it!

NASA accomplished their 'moon shot' on 20th July 1969, holding Kennedy to his word: putting a man on the moon before the end of the decade. In all, 12 men set foot on the moon between 1969 - 1972.

What a huge vision. What an amazing accomplishment!

Or take Sir Ernest Shackleton, who in August 1914 set sail on the Endurance with the BHAG of taking a team to the South Pole. Just one day away from their intended destination the ship got stuck fast in the ice and was eventually crushed, leaving the men to camp on an ice floe for 18 months in sub-zero temperatures. Ravaged by Antarctic storms, twelve hundred miles from the nearest civilisation, Shackleton abandoned his original vision of reaching the South Pole in favour of an even more implausible and audacious goal: to get every one of his men home alive. If you've every read anything about polar exploring, you'll realise how ludicrous that vision was.

Having run out of supplies after being stranded for well

over a year in a desolate and remote part of the world, the chances of survival for any individual was slim. For all of them it was an impossibility, but that was the BHAG that Shackleton set before himself and his team. The amazing part of it was that because of the culture that Shackleton had built, his men actually dared to believe him! Even after a year on the ice, they were still in good spirits believing in the impossible hope of return.

However, nearly three years after they left Britain, Shackleton took a small crew in a twenty-foot lifeboat and attempted the treacherous trip of 800 miles across the most stormy stretch of ocean in the world facing waves of up to fifty foot in height.

Then, on the 17 August 1917, Shackleton returned and rescued his entire crew. Not a single person was lost.

Now that's a BHAG! An almost impossible vision of the future that rallies people to achieve above and beyond what they ever thought possible.

Does your organisation have a vision? A BHAG? A picture of an impossible future that might just be reachable?

A properly set out compelling vision will draw your

potentially disparate teams and departments together to pull in the same direction and helps to regulate what projects and activities the organisation gets involved in. And conversely what the organisation leaves and ignores.

Take Apple in 1997 when it's founder, who was fired in 1985, came back to save the company.

In the year immediately preceding Steve Jobs' return to Apple the computer company had made a $1.04 billion loss and when he took over as CEO they were just 90 days from bankruptcy. Three CEOs had come and gone in a decade. Board members had tried to sell the company but found no takers.

Within a year the company posted a $300 million profit.

The first thing Jobs did when he returned was to rationalise the products and set a vision of creating a few stunningly beautiful, exceptional products. He inspired his team to create something that no one could emulate saying, "If we do our jobs right, no one else should be able to do what we can do. We should be in an incredible place as this convergence of computing and communications explodes in the next few years."

His vision and focus took Apple from an also-ran computer company to the biggest company in the world (based on market capitalisation) and probably the most successful brand in the history.

A great vision focuses, inspires, gathers and challenges people to come together to reach for the future they only glimpse.

To truly have the right impact your vision needs to be three things:

Almost out of reach. A good vision is far enough away that it is a challenge, but close enough that people can see that it just might be possible.

Short. People should be able to remember it easily. Like the mission, if it's more than a couple of sentences, it's too complicated.

Inspiring. It needs to evoke an emotional response and be something that people can connect with on more than a rational level if they are to put time, energy and heart into making it real.

One of best examples of an inspiring vision is from Oxfam,

the international charity which sees the future as "a just world without poverty." It's short, memorable, easy to understand, evokes an emotive response that draws me in and most importantly it is big, very, very big!

So what is it that your organisation is going to do? How do you see the future ten years from now? What's your moon shot? Use the next few pages to think it through and note down some ideas.

Once you have your purpose - Mission, Values, Vision - you have a 'raison d'etre' that will inspire, challenge and motive. You have the simple cry to rally people.

Now let's take a look at who those people are.

You know what to do...

What does your world look like in 10 years time? What impact has your organisation had in that time?

How will you be remembered after that time? What will people be saying about you?

What do you want the future to look like?

WHO'S IN
WHO'S OUT?

"Great things in business are never done by one person.
They are done by a team of people."

STEVE JOBS

In the early 1980s, the Ford Motor Company was not enjoying its previously heady success. It was losing money - $3.3 billion over three years – to its cheaper and more efficient Japanese competitors, like Toyota. In 1983 they set about trying to stem the slide and restore the fortunes of the 80 year old prestigious motor company. The first step made by the management team at the time was to clarify exactly what it was that Ford Motor Company stood for. They began redefining the mission, values and guiding principles (a document that later become known as MVGP) - a great start.

However, during this process of purpose definition they discovered something that had been overlooked for some time by the organisation in it's period of decline, something which had been at the heart of Henry Ford's original, founding vision. Don Peterson, the former CEO, recalls that during this period of reframing, "there was a great deal of talk about the sequence of the three Ps – people, products and profits. It was decided that people should absolutely come first."

Getting the right people "on the bus", as Jim Collins puts

it, is vitally important to the success of your organisation. Without the right people, inspired and released to work in their sweet spot, your organisation is not going to be all that it can be. Often, even a slight change in the composition of your team can make a radical difference in its ability to perform. Whether good or bad, people will impact your organisation's ability to execute its mission and it's imperative to get the right people.

The second thing Steve Jobs did on his return to Apple, after setting a new vision, mentioned in the previous chapter, was to change his management team and bring in people who got his vision and shared his passion. Within a few weeks of taking over Jobs managed to force the resignation of most of Apple's board members. He put Jonathan Ive in charge of design and he brought in Tim Cook, Compaq's self-styled "Attila the Hun of inventory," to run manufacturing. He understood that if he wanted to turn Apple round and build the company he envisioned, then he needed the right people to do it.

"Any strategy, no matter how smart, is dead on arrival unless a company brings it to life with people – the right people."

JACK WELCH

But, if it's important to have the right people, who exactly are the right people?

PEOPLE WHO CATCH THE PURPOSE

"There are many things that will catch my eye, but there are only a few things that will catch my heart."

TIM REDMOND

When choosing the right people you need to hire people who believe in what you are trying to build. People who share your passion and are willing to put their shoulder to the plough of your mission and vision. People who buy into what you are trying to build and get as excited as you do about it. Firstly, people with that level of enthusiasm for the mission will do the job with a similar passion and focus that you would yourself and secondly they will need far less management and intervention in the process!

You see, you can't really get people to do what you need with just a monetary reward! Daniel Pink describes experiments which uncovered an interesting and counter intuitive phenomenon when it comes to paying people: financial reward actually has an adverse impact on performance. Put simply, the more you pay someone, the worse the person's performance gets. It seems that the pressure to have to perform actually undermines a person's ability to perform. The bigger the reward the more worried a person gets about expectations, limiting their risk and creativity, reducing the overall accomplishment. The out-working of this is that you can't make someone do a task well just for monetary compensation.

If you start your career when you're 21 and work through to the current UK retirement age of 65, you will work for 44 years. For each year that you work, you will spend about 228 days in the office, which equates to more than 10,000 days in your lifetime. At a standard eight hours a days, that's over 80,000 hours of work. An awful lot of hours of your life to invest in something. Is it worth it just for money? No! You can't pay someone to deliver enthusiastic excellence and if you can't get the best from a person by simply paying them more, how do you get a team to perform to their peak?

Obviously, you need to give them some other reason to do what you're asking. You need to appeal to their emotions. You need to capture their heart with a compelling and challenging picture of the future. You need to give their work meaning with a mission and vision that inspires them.

Ultimately, you need them to *catch* your purpose and buy into what you're building.

In The 8th Habit, Stephen Covey suggests that we all desire to have unique personal significance; what Covey calls voice. Our voice, which motivates us to a higher level of performance, occurs when four things come together: our passion, our talent, our need and our conscience. Satisfying need alone, with financial reward, is not sufficient to inspire us to do our best work. To truly do great work we must release our passion (that which energises and inspires us); we must appeal to our conscience (that small, internal voice that assures us we are doing good); and we must employ our talent (that which we were born to do).

James Stillman, president of Citicorp at the turn of the last century, fully understood the benefits of gathering a team that were passionate about a shared vision:

"Stillman intended [Citicorp] to retain its position [as the largest and strongest bank in the US] even after his death, and to ensure this he filled the new building with people who shared his own vision and entrepreneurial spirit."

CITIBANK 1812 – 1970

James Stillman built an institution that could continue without him and more than 100 years later Citigroup (a successor to Citicorp) sits at number 20 on the Fortune 500 list, with a 4% increase in profits in 2011. Not too shabby for a bank during a recession!

But not all organisations have a leader like Stillman. A Gallup poll in the U.S. taken in 2011 showed that 71% of workers were emotionally disengaged from their workplace and as a result were less productive which, Gallup estimated, cost businesses a staggering $350 billion every year; that's $2,246 per disengaged employee. And that figure doesn't even take into account the impact a single disengaged employee has on the culture of an organisation. After all, misery is contagious!

The key thing about purpose is that you can't teach it. You can't train someone to be passionate about your purpose. You can't pay them to see what you can see. You can run a weekend retreat and get people fired up. You can deliver a rousing speech and inspire people, but you can't create a long term, day-in-day-out connection with a mission through training. People either connect or they don't. So don't waste your money or your time, hire people in the first instance that already catch the purpose.

Edward Deci, a university psychology graduate student in 1969, wrote that people have an "inherent tendency to seek out novelty and challenges, to extend and exercise their capabilities, to explore, and to learn." If you can give employees a compelling vision in which to exercise that 'inherent tendency', then you will be surprised what someone will achieve and you will save yourself time, effort and money in having to manage and organise them. (But we'll get to that part a little later.)

For instance, consider Valve, a game development company with an extremely flat management structure. According to their handbook for new employees, subtitled, 'A fearless adventure in knowing what to do when no one's there telling you what to do',

> "...there is no hierarchy. When you're an entertainment company that's spent the last decade going out of its way to recruit the most intelligent, innovative, talented

people on Earth, telling them to sit at a desk and do what they're told obliterates 99 percent of their value. We want innovators, and that means maintaining an environment where they'll flourish...This company is yours to steer—toward opportunities and away from risks."

VALVE HANDBOOK

The future of the company is directly in the hands of the people they hired. People that catch the vision. People who have built Valve up to a $2 billion company.

People who catch the purpose are your best asset, but once you're sure they see what you see, make sure they also fit the culture.

PEOPLE WHO FIT THE CULTURE

"A culture may be conceived as a network of beliefs and purposes in which any string in the net pulls and is pulled by the others, thus perpetually changing the configuration of the whole."

JACQUES BARZUNI

Let's jump back to our old school friend who came to

dinner at the beginning of this book. How did you feel? Did you ignore him, or were you polite? Did you immediately ask him to leave, or feign tiredness and encourage him to leave without a scene? You created a culture in your home (it may not have been explicit, but it's there) and when it was violated by your guest, it caused problems.

When someone comes in and cuts across that culture, the atmosphere gets strained.

And so it is within your organisation. Your culture is the system of shared values, behaviours and beliefs about what's important and appropriate in your organisation. Whether you've deliberately created it or it has organically grown by default, inviting someone into this environment who does not share the same cultural values and beliefs will cause friction, in the same way as the rude dinner guest did in your house. Just as one bad apple spoils the batch, so one person who does not choose to accept and live by an organisation's values can undermine the entire culture and atmosphere, unsettling the rest of your team.

Along with catching the vision, the people you let into your organisation need to share the values too. You need to be sure that they are not only happy behaving as you would want them to behave, but they do it automatically. It's part of who they are. They implicitly share your cultural values.

I once worked for an organisation that was growing rapidly and adding a number of people to their head office team. I was hired to improve their online presence and increase the usability of their e-commerce site. It was a great organisation with a friendly, encouraging and supportive culture. The management team seemed to hire people they trusted and allow them the freedom to do their jobs well. A lot of the people on the management team had come up through the organisation and learnt on the job. They were a brilliant bunch of people who loved what they do. *(And still do – most of them are still there!)* They worked hard and played hard, enjoying regular social events together.

Shortly after I arrived, a new senior manager was hired, who became my line manager. He was a great guy socially, and very skilled at the role he'd been hired into. I learnt a lot from him and still keep in touch via social media. However, he also struggled with insecurities as to whether he was good enough, and under pressure he got stressed, depressed and angry. At times this would manifest it's self in belittling others, getting defensive and argumentative and putting unnecessary pressure on his direct reports (of which I was one!).

As you can imagine, the culture changed somewhat, certainly from my vantage point. I struggled to do my best work, always concerned about whether what I was doing was right or would be good enough. It was a tough period for me, for my boss and for the company. Eventually, after about two years, the management took a really hard decision and he had to be let go for the sake of the organisation. No matter how skilled a person may be, if they don't fit the culture it's not worth hiring them. It will always cost you in the end.

Like vision, you can't teach someone *their* values or train them to fit the culture you've built, you can only assess if they match. You need to make sure that no one gets past the gate who doesn't already fit your organisation's culture. It takes a lot of effort and time to build an organisational culture. Don't risk disrupting it. No matter how skilled or talented a prospective employee appears, if they don't fit the culture, don't hire them.

CULTURE TRUTH #4

You can train someone for skill, but it's far more difficult to change someone's heart and passion!

When Jack Welch was CEO of General Electric, he presided over a team of leaders who grew the organisation by 4000%, in multiple markets across the globe. He knew a thing or two about hiring the right kind of people. In his book Winning, Jack clearly outlines the framework that he used to decide whether or not a person was suitable to work at GE. The framework assessed a person in eight areas: integrity, intelligence, maturity, energy, energising others, courage, ability to execute and passion. The unusual thing about this list, especially in light of the world class nature of the organisation, is that only two out of the eight areas relate to skill – intelligence and ability to execute. The other six are all related to the person's character. Seventy five percent of Jack's selection process focused on discovering who a person was rather than what they could do. He was clearly more concerned to discover whether a person would fit the organisation's culture.

According to Edgar Schein, a professor at MIT Sloan School of Management, "The only thing of real importance that leaders do is to create and manage culture." Whether or not you agree that it's the only thing a leader does, it is certainly one of the most important aspects of leadership. Moreover, one thing a leader does need to do is ensure that nothing interferes with the culture they want to foster within the organisation.

Herb Kelleher, founder of Southwest Airlines, believed that you should hire primarily for character and attitude rather than skill. He always maintained that once you had the right person, you could always train them to improve their skill, but it's nearly impossible to change a person's character. To mould someone to the inherent culture is extemely difficult and takes time, effort and money. Be deliberate about building your culture and hire people with the character that fits.

Or take a lead from Zappos, the billion dollar online shoe retailer. Zappos are so fervent about ensuring they employ the right people, that one week into their 4 week induction, they offer each new employee $2000 to quit there and then. It may sound excessive, but it ensures that the only people who get inside their organisation are people who share their passion and actually want to work for them. It is a simple mechanism that protects the culture that Tony Hseih, the CEO, has meticulously crafted.

In order to keep politics out of your organisation, you must protect your culture at all costs with the right people. And when you have the right people, you also need just the right leaders.

LEADERS

"If you can't influence others they won't follow you. And if they won't follow you, you're not a leader."

JACK WELCH

In his best-selling book, The 21 Irrefutable Laws of Leadership, John Maxwell recalls a sobering but extremely visual demonstration of leadership: "Occasionally," he writes "you hear of four military jets crashing while flying in formation." Maxwell explains that when jet fighters fly in formation, one of the pilots is designated the leader. The leader defines everything: where the formation flies; what altitude they fly at; what speed they fly at; what manoeuvres they perform. Whatever manoeuvres the leader makes the other planes flying on his wing also make: "This is true whether he soars in the clouds or crashes into a mountaintop."

Anyway you look at it, leaders will have a profound effect on the success or failure of an organisation; "Everything rises and falls on leadership." The leaders bring an organisation to life. For better or for worse your leaders colour your whole organisation, so choose them very carefully.

Firstly, recognise that leadership is not about title or position in an organisation. Leadership is simply about influence. As Jack Welch puts it, "if you can't influence others they won't follow you. And if they won't follow you, you're not a leader." Good leaders know this. They don't hold their position highly, but they do protect their relationships with integrity and loyalty.

Make sure your leaders are people who can build and maintain relationships well. If necessary get rid of titles and hierarchy, true leaders do not need them to successfully lead.

"Being in power is like being a lady. If you have to tell people you are, you aren't"

MARGARET THATCHER

Secondly, great leaders are able to build and engender trust. Trust turns a good team into a great team. Where there is genuine trust, a team can work unfettered by the shadow of organisational politics; agendas do not need to be questioned; information does not get hoarded; people are free to excel in their own sphere and to work together for the common good. Great leaders can create that trust within a team and take a group of individuals of average skill to the level of a high performing team. Just ask the Greek football team, who in 2004 achieved what is probably still the biggest shock in football, beating the favoured hosts, Portugal to win the European Championship.

Greece was a team of average players without a single household name, taking on the might of Cristiano Ronaldo and Luis Figo, who was, at the time, the most expensive footballer in the world. But what Otto Rehhagel, the Greek coach managed to do was get a group of average individuals to play above themselves as a high performing team, beating a much more skilled group of world class individuals.

One of the key ways that leaders build trust is by serving. Great leaders are able to subordinate their ego for the greater good: "It's not that they have no ego or self-interest. Indeed, they are incredibly ambitious – but their ambition is first and foremost for the institution, not themselves." The leaders you are looking for have the strength to surround themselves with people smarter and more skilled than they are themselves, people who know better. They are not intimidated by other people's success or ability. They are able to put their whole focus on doing everything they can to make sure their team can perform and succeed.

> "The best executive is the one who has the sense
> enough to pick good men to do what he wants done
> and the self-restraint enough to keep from meddling with
> them while they do it."

THEODORE ROOSEVELT

As one longtime employee at Hewlett Packard put it, "I have the impression that Bill [Hewlett] and Dave [Packard] work for me, rather than the other way around." And Nordstrom, the clothing retailer, has an organisational chart that's an upside down pyramid with the board of directors at the bottom, serving the staff, who serve the customer.

Thirdly, great leaders live and breathe the mission, vision and values of an organisation and by this they set the culture and expectations within the organisation. Every person in your organisation must be infused with the company DNA; they must grasp and live out the mission and vision of the organisation but the leaders are the ones who make that happen. For them it must become a mantra; a constant CD on single track repeat. They must return to it regularly. They must communicate it in all interactions – verbally and non-verbally. They must become the living embodiment of the mission, values and vision of the organisation. In doing so, people will be inspired to copy them.

Jack Welch believes that the formation of the mission, vision and values of the organisation can only be set by the leadership. It cannot be delegated and must come from the leadership. It must be part of who they are as individuals and as a leadership team. Like the rest of your team, leaders must catch the vision. They must fit the culture, but they are a special breed. When hiring leaders you should look for people who don't care for title, who build trust and who are as maniacal about the mission, values and vision of your organisation as you are!

A word of warning: while it is important that you hire people who catch your purpose and fit the culture; people who share you values, be careful not to hire people who always agree with you. A healthy organisation fosters debate and disagreement. Discourse is good and ensures all decisions are robust and stand up to proper scrutiny. This cannot happen with a team of people looking to agree with the CEO. People must be confident enough and be allowed room enough to disagree and discuss issues until a decision is made. They then need to be committed enough, once a decision has been made, to execute as if it was their choice in the first place. This is how the most successful teams operate.

So, choose your leaders wisely, they play a big part in developing the voice of your organisation, which we will look at next.

Do your thing

Who in your organisations best exemplifies the culture you want to build? What qualities does that person have that you think reflects the culture? Are there individuals in your organisation that don't reflect the culture well? How will you manage those people? What things need to change? What character traits should you be looking for when hiring new people into your company?

WHAT'S THAT
YOU SAY?

"But if thought corrupts language,
language can also corrupt thought."

GEORGE ORWELL

Have you ever met someone famous?   Not just randomly bumped into them and taken a selfie, but actually specifically met someone famous to have a decent conversation with them. Someone you'd seen many times on the screen and in the press.   Someone you'd formed a particular opinion about in your mind from what you'd seen and read. Someone you perhaps looked up to.

Have you met them in the flesh and had a real conversation with them, only to find out that the image you held of them is completely false. Once you finally spent time with them, you realised they were nothing like you expected them to be.

Generally, people in the public eye have PR firms and advisors to help them portray a specific image. Some of them work very hard on creating a public persona and they do this for many reasons, some good and some not so good.   However, sometimes, those facades are just that, fake!   The tabloids are full of stories and incidents that show when the cracks appear and the "real" person starts to show.

We tend not to like it when that happens. We tend not to like them when it happens. We tend to judge people quite harshly.

There are some celebrities, however, who are exactly as you'd expect them to be. Individuals who "walk the talk". The ones whose public image matches their private character. The ones who practise what they preach. These are the people we long admire. The ones that the tabloid don't write about. (Probably because it doesn't sell newspapers.) Those are the ones we look up to. They are consistent in what they say and what they do. People with integrity. Authentic people.

There is a wonderful story about Keanu Reeves who was attending the wrap-up party for the film 'Daughter of God' that had just finished filming and in which he'd been the lead actor. The bouncer at the club where the party was held didn't recognise him and kept him waiting outside for 20 minutes until his friends arrived. He didn't complain and was so relaxed about the incident that he didn't even mention it to the organiser of the party. He just patiently waited until he was allowed in and let the bouncer do the job he was there to do.

It's not just celebrities. We've all met people, spoken to

people and spent time with people who talk a good story but don't behave consistently with what they say. People who don't "walk the talk". We find them untrustworthy. We don't give them respect. We're sceptical of what they say and we don't trust what they do. They are inauthentic and we are unlikely to follow with any enthusiasm, even if they are our boss, our designated leader or pay our wages.

Unfortunately, it's exactly the same with organisations.

How many times have you seen the marketing from phone companies, espousing how great they are with their customers, only to call up and discover the reality does not match the rhetoric? **"Press 1 for billing; Press 2 for Support; Press 3 for......."**

It's not long before we have to find an outlet for our frustrations and that usually involves complaining to those around us about how poor the organisation is.

When did you last call an online retailer to sort out an order gone awry only to talk to someone who didn't listen, didn't understand or didn't care, despite the façade of the company saying how much they want to make their customers' lives easier.

A health insurance company, for example, created an advertising campaign letting everyone know that the "welfare of patients" was the company's absolute top priority, but, when talking with employees, their view on the inside was that their main goal was to increase the value of their stock options through cost reductions.

If you want to build a consistent, authentic culture which people trust and relate to (both internally and externally) then what you say and how you communicate internally - **your organisation's voice** - is massively important and has to match the way you've articulated how you want to behave.   It has to be consistent with the rest of the defined purpose. It has to match all the other things you say, otherwise you are merely one of our inauthentic, disrespected celebrities with a facade building PR machine. No one really wants to work in that organisation and customers only do business with them if they lack options. We can all list companies we've dealt with that fit this description.

CULTURE TRUTH #5

*What you say must match how you behave
to create a truly authentic culture.*

But when you get it right....

When your voice and your actions do match up, when what you say throughout your organisation over time shows consistency, it all adds weight to your trustworthiness and authenticity and creates a legion of loyal customers and employees.

It truly builds a brilliant, effective and authentic culture, where people love to work and what customers choose to talk about.

There are so many areas in organisational life that are included in this idea of voice and they all need to be consistent with each other as well as with the behaviour of the organisation.   It starts with the purpose that you've already defined and moves through the policies that it enacts; the way the leadership communicates with staff; how staff members communicate with one another; the way you speak to each other in meetings; the company branding and marketing collateral; the colours you use on the website; the imagery you associate with your organisation; the way emails are used; the way you answer the phone; whether there is a human or computer on the end of the line; your holiday policy and flexible working arrangements; your hiring (and firing) process; the dress code; the employee perks - and so much more. All these things need to be thought through proactively so they are consistent and reinforce the organisational purpose.

Famously Albert Mehrabian, did some research into the relative importance or words vs tone vs body language when talking about feelings and attitude. He discovered that only 7% was communicated by words, 38% by tone of voice and 55% by body language. In a similar way, when trying to engage with employees and customers emotionally, there are lots of different factors that have different impact in that communication. The key thing to get right is consistency across all of them.

When these things are not consistent and don't continually say the same thing, visually, verbally, in written form or however, then people notice and it makes them uncomfortable. They start to lose trust. People may not be able to explain why they feel that way, but they intuitively feel that there is something wrong, something of which to be wary. Something untrustworthy and it will impact their relationship with the organisation. The culture will be tainted.

This is also the area where you can exercise the most

control, allowing you to shape the relationship that the company has with its staff and, by extension, the way customers interact with your company

Most organisations understand the importance of branding in the external marketing sense - making sure customers view your organisation in the right way, consistent with who you are. It is equally important, however, to ensure that every internal interaction and the impact it has needs to be thought through carefully to ensure that it reflects and reinforces the purpose of your organisation if you want to build a consistent and true culture.

It is so important to spend time on this area, because it helps employees to make a powerful emotional connection to what your organisation does. Without that connection, employees are likely to undermine the purpose, values, expectations and culture that you are trying to build. In some cases, this is because they simply don't understand what you've defined so they end up working at cross-purposes. In other cases, it may be they don't actually believe in the purpose and feel disengaged or, worse, hostile toward the company.

It seems obvious that when employees care about and

believe in the mission they are motivated to work harder and their loyalty to the company increases. Employees are unified and inspired by a common sense of purpose and identity.

Unfortunately, internal branding and culture building is often none existent or done poorly. While leaders understand the need to keep people informed about the company's strategy and direction, few understand the need or the power of language and internal voice to build an inspiring and coherent culture. What's more, the people who are charged with internal communications are usually HR professionals and often don't have the marketing skills to communicate the purpose effectively. Information is communicated in memos, emails and newsletters, but no one has thought about how to inspire with what they are really part of.

Like the purpose, without specific attention, ways of communicating, interacting and engaging will grow organically. As an organisational leader you need to define the internal language and interactions so they reinforce and reflect the purpose. This way you will be building a truly authentic culture.

If you wouldn't use a generic off the shelf advert to

communicate your brand to your customers, why would you use generic communication for your staff? Ultimately, the relationship you have with your staff is far more important, since it is they who ultimately define the success of your company and communicates the culture to your clients and customers. It is, therefore, an area that companies ignore at their peril, weakening their relationship with their staff and ultimately damaging not only their ability to retain talent but their productivity and their bottom line as well.

So ask yourself the question what are you really saying to people? What is in that 55% of communication that your organisation speaks? Choose to be deliberate about every area of your company's voice, because once you have this well defined it becomes easy to create One Focus....

Let's think about one aspect of voice. How does your organisation answer the phone to customers? If you were the customer and that's how the phone was answered to you, how would you feel? Is that an emotion you want associated with your company brand? What could you do change that emotion to better fit your organisation? Think about other areas of interaction in your organisation.

WHAT HAPPENED
IN HERE?

"Things that matter most must never be at the mercy of things that matter least."

JOHANN WOLFGANG VON GOETHE

I once heard a story about a successful management consultant who was invited into a large organisation to work with their sales team. The new sales director had been in post for four months and needed some help to solve a very specific issue with his team. The sales team at the organisation were performing reasonably well. Since the new Sales Director started all the numbers had gone in the right direction, but the new guy had high standards and big growth targets that he expected his team to hit. He felt there was more that could be done. If the sales team would collaborate and work together more, supporting one another, then the results would not just be good, they'd be spectacular. He'd break all targets.

His main focus over the last 3 months had been to increase co-operation and team work within the sales team. He had tried just about everything to motivate his team to come together, none of which seemed to have much impact on the level of co-operation.

He'd given speeches about teamwork. He got rid of offices and moved everyone in to an open plan space. He had publicly recognised and praised the few who had occasionally (and reluctantly) worked together. He'd organised regular after work socialising. Up to this point not a single thing had had the desired impact on getting his team to collaborate. Nothing seemed to be very effective at all.

"I don't know what I'm missing," he told the consultant, "but I don't seem to be able to get them to support each other or work together."

The consultant sat quietly in the Sales Director's office and listened carefully to this tale of woe, all the while looking around his well appointed office and taking in his surroundings.

When the sales director had finished and sat slumped in his chair, almost resigned to that fact that there was nothing that could be done, the consultant looked up and pointed to a huge chart he'd noticed on the wall behind the director's desk. It filled almost the entire wall behind the desk and on it were a list of names, with varying scales of numbers next to each one. To the right of the chart was a beautiful picture of a golden beach, somewhere in the tropics - the Bahamas perhaps.

"What's that?" the consultant asked.

The sales director who, up until this point, remained downcast and seemed lost in his predicament, suddenly came alive and smiled proudly. "That," he exclaimed, "is my masterpiece. It's the league table of each sales person's performance. We keep a tally of all of the sales and the best performing sales person at the end of the quarter wins a trip to Bermuda. Everyone loves it."

It seems fairly simple, when hearing a story like that, to figure out that, while his team are competing against each other for a trip to Bermuda, they're never going to help each other. One man's loss is another man's gain. There is no benefit to helping each other. In fact it's self sabotaging to help someone else. This Sales Director was never going to get his team to collaborate until he changed what he measured and what he rewarded. A lot of organisations, however, seem happy to operate in exactly this way.   They articulate a mission, values and vision that they aspire to, but their actions and the way the organisation behaves not only don't reflect those aspirations, but often actively work against them.

I've already mentioned earlier in the book about organisations who talk a good game, but the reality is sorely lacking. They espouse a very laudable purpose, yet seem to struggle to live it out at the coalface. The reason for this incongruence is simple. The way the members of that organisation behave doesn't reinforce the mission, vision and values that have been articulated They are inauthentic - say one thing and do something different. In the same way this sales director's behaviour does not reinforce his stated goal of collaboration.

As we've already discovered, the key to becoming a culture without politics and hidden agendas, a culture of high performance, is to make sure your mission, vision and values (MVV) become the reality of your organisation. Once you have your MVV established, you need to take time to ensure that this purpose and the underlying values permeate every area of your business, from the physical space that your customers see to the metrics you measure; from the structures and teams you create to the processes you write; from the remuneration you offer to the behaviours you reward and the behaviours you sanction. Your articulated purpose is only truly your purpose if every part of your organisation lives, breathes and reinforces it.

Like the proverbial stick of British seaside rock the MVV should be written all the way through your organisation, and every part of your organisation should reflect the same MVV. This ensures you create an organistion founded on integrity and established with potential for real and lasting success. You truly practice what you preach and become an authentic, politic-free organisation.

Everything must flow from this foundation.

We already know that every organisation has a mission, core values and vision, whether they are explicit and deliberately cultivated or left to organically develop. Every organisation's purpose and culture is expressed through the collective actions of its teams, not through words in a corporate document.   Even if you have spent hours defining and articulating what you believe your mission, values and vision to be, unless they are lived out in the behaviours and attitudes of the people in your organisation, they are nothing more than wishful thinking. The truly active purpose of your organisation is cultivated through developing the right systems and environment to establish behaviours and attitudes that match your aspirations.

To become an authentic and politic-free culture you should be very deliberate about designing your metrics and rewards; your policies and procedures; your space and environment, to express and reflect your very core values and mission, or your organisation will fail to deliver on its articulated raison d'etre. Don't let that happen. Be as deliberate about the functional parts of your organisation as you have been about the purpose.

STRATEGY, METRICS & REWARDS

"The purpose of compensation should not be to get the right behaviours from the wrong people, but to get the right people on the bus in the first place and keep them there."

JIM COLLINS

Our sales director story is quite a simplistic example of a prevalent organisational phenomenon. This issue often exists in organisations in more hidden ways and is not always as obvious to identify. I've seen it many times in more subtle ways – companies articulating a laudable mission and inspiring core values only to undermine them with their systems of management information and compensation. Jim Collins' study in Good to Great found that a lot of organisations have great intentions and inspiring visions but not only fail to translate this intention into a concrete strategy, they even tolerate tactics, characteristics and strategies that push against their mission and values.

Your strategy, metrics, rewards and incentives must be fully aligned with the purpose and values and designed to encourage the behaviours and culture you're creating.

If incentives are all geared towards individual reward, then who's going to co-operate? If they are all directed at delivering the monthly sales numbers, will anyone act for the longer term goals? If you focus your strategy on increasing client numbers can you ensure your customer service values will be met? If you measure working hours, but not quality and volume of work, people will be on time and possibly work long hours, but are unlikely to deliver their best work. If your strategic focus is to increase retention, does it fit with your vision of growth?

Quite simply, defining and articulating your mission, vision and values, is a total waste of time unless it is backed up by organisational practices that put them at the heart of the organisation. In order to make the mission, vision and values the heart of an organisation, you must build the strategy, metrics and rewards around them.

Firstly, you obviously need to think about strategy. Many management tome has been penned on how to develop effective strategy, and to be honest, this is the part that many organisation seem to do well. It is a key part of any

MBA programme. In his book 'The Advantage', Patrick Lencioni asks a question to help organisations figure out their current focus - what he calls the strategic anchors. He simply asks, "What is most important right now? What do we need to do over the next 12 - 18 months to move towards our goal?" The key phrase here is "to move towards our goal". Whatever strategic anchors you decide are important they absolutely must be consistent with your organisational mission. They must not step outside the constraints set by the organisational values and they must move the organisation towards it's stated vision.

After this, whatever management information you decide you need to effectively report on your strategic progress and run your organisation should be designed to inform you whether or not you are working out your mission, how consistent you are with your core values and demonstrate whether you are moving towards your vision. Does your management reporting give you enough information to decide whether progress has been made towards the vision? Can you see the results of time and effort spent on the strategic anchors? Are you able to see good progress on the current vision?

If your MI does not allow you to answer these questions

(alongside the day to day questions of sales, cashflow, P&L etc) then you need to improve your metrics. If your mission and vision are not reflected in the reporting that you receive, then either your metrics are wrong or you haven't really defined your MVV correctly.

Secondly, whatever compensation, benefit and system of praise you implement should reward those people who execute the mission well and behave consistently with the desired values and strategic anchors. Moreover, it should sanction those who contravene the values and fail to work towards the vision.

Let's go back to our sales director with the 'trip to Bahamas' incentive. Perhaps one of his best sales people is Jennifer. Over the period she consistently sells more, 18% more than any other sales person and she always breaks her target with time to spare in the month. She is first into the office everyday and often last out. Measured by those facts, Jennifer is a top employee. She should be well compensated and she more than deserves to win the trip. Go Jennifer! Would you want to hire Jennifer into your sales team? Probably.

You might want to wait just a second before you offer her a contract. On the one hand Jennifer hits all the right numbers and seems to be the ideal candidate, but what if I told you that Jennifer's manager is constantly getting complaints about her from other team members? Sour grapes? Perhaps, but apparently she arrives early and leaves late, so that she can cherry pick the leads she calls. She even calls leads from other sales people and steals their sales. She is underhand and rude to her team mates and many good employees have cited her behaviour in exit interviews as a contributing factor to their leaving. Couple that with the fact that the clients she brings in are often poor quality, they don't remain clients long and they are difficult and expensive to manage, leaving little margin in working for them.

Would you still want to take her on? Do you still think she deserves the reward of a trip to the Bahamas? If she does, then over time everyone else on your team will start to behave the same way. Everyone will start to copy the behaviours of the people that are praised.

Do you still want to hire her? Or more importantly, imagine managing a team of Jennifers, which is exactly what will happen if her sales numbers alone dictate the rewards. How might you adjust your metrics to ensure that you incorporated some way to assess the hidden depths of Jennifer's abilities? How could you ensure that your rewards and metrics reflect the values that you have created for your organisation?

CULTURE TRUTH #6

What you measure and the behaviours you praise or punish will become your culture.

It's also important to remember that your reward system should not be just about financial gain. Do you recall what we said about Daniel Pink's research? He demonstrated that money only motivates for non-cerebral menial tasks – the more you pay the better the outcome for those simple tasks - but once the tasks involve rudimentary cognitive skill, the more you pay, the poorer the outcome of those tasks. Pay your people enough for money not to be a factor and then find other ways to reward them. Ways that demonstrate your commitment to them and reinforce your MVV.

"Those acts motivated by emotional rewards are most consistently performed."

PADDI LUND

You can choose to be very creative with your system of

recognition and rewards. For example, you might try more flexible working; or leaving hand written notes on your teams' desks; maybe organise special events; give high performers surprise and random extra days off; give out monopoly money that can be exchanged for gifts and treats. Whatever works for your people, as long as it constantly reiterates and rewards those in line with the mission, values and vision of your organisation.

Your rewards system should also be as simple and non-bureacratic as possible. Which brings us to the next part - 'polices and procedures.'

POLICIES & PROCEDURE

"Relentlessly seek out the best practices to achieve your big a-ha, whether inside or out, adapt them and continually improve them."

JACK WELCH

If you were writing a unofficial handbook for new recruits at your organisation what would it include? How big would it be? How many dos and don'ts would it contain? Would it match the official one that your organisation gives to new starters? What would it say to the Jennifers of this world?

For many years, new recruits at Nordstrom, an American upscale fashion retailer, were given a simple 5-by-8-inch card containing just 75 words:

"Welcome to Nordstrom. We're glad to have you with our Company. Our number one goal is to provide outstanding customer service. Set both your personal and professional goals high. We have great confidence in your ability to achieve them.

Nordstrom Rules: Rule #1: Use best judgment in all situations. There will be no additional rules.

Please feel free to ask your department manager, store manager, or division general manager any question at any time."

At Nordstrom, employees aren't just given responsibility, they are given authority too. They are given permission to do their job within the confines of the Nordstrom mission and values to provide outstanding customer service but they are free to decide how best to do their job.

This is the heart of what it means to hire a team that gets

the mission. A community of like-minded people with a passion, freed to be brilliant at what they do. But it's not easy to accomplish in today's world. Times have changed. Business is now only just catching up.

At the turn of the nineteenth century the world was based around an agricultural economy. Farmers had livestock and grew produce, trading them nationally and globally. Economics were simple and obvious. Then, during the nineteenth century, all that changed and the world moved into the industrial age. Factories sprang up, manufacturing thrived and people moved from the fields to the cities.

During the Industrial Age, the key to success was efficiency and the most valuable assets were the means of production – the expensive machines. People were needed to operate the machines, but not to think or make decisions. All they needed to do was simply follow the prescribed procedures. People were a resource, but they were not assets. A lot of medium to large businesses are still living in this epoch of thinking. Unfortunately, their employees are not.

Commerce has moved into the Information Age, where people ARE the means of production - the expensive machines of the Industrial Age. People are now valuable assets and need to be released to produce. However, many organisations still work to the paradigm of the Industrial Age, where workers are nothing more than resources who follow instructions. Unfortunately, this system will no longer produce the best results. Like Nordstrom, organisations need to recognise their workers as assets and set them free to perform.

As Theodore Malloch points out "critics of capitalism in the last century did not deny that the industrial revolution had drastically increased wealth, but that it had reduced individuals to an impersonal cog in the wealth machine." Too many policies and procedures in large organisations continue to make this a reality, with people reduced to cogs or simply a usable resource in the HR database.

Jack Welch once shared a significant epiphany when he had an unexpected conversation with one employee who told him "for twenty five years you paid for my hands when you could have had my brain as well – for nothing."

People are not just unemotional resources. In fact the alternative is actually much simpler to manage if we can get it right. Hire the right people and trust them to do what needs to be done.

If we can get our recruitment processes correct and ensure that we have people who are not only skilled for the role, but also share a passion for the missions, values and vision, and fit the culture of our organisation, then we are unlikely to have to resort to creating reams of regulating policies and procedures, just to keep them drifting outside of our expected behaviours.

Jim Nordstrom, CEO and the grandson of Nordstrom's founder, was once questioned in a Stanford Business School class about what his staff would do if a customer attempted to return a dress that had clearly been worn. His answer sums up what it means to employ the right people and cut them loose to do the right thing with authority and responsibility:

> "I don't know. That's the honest answer. But I do have a high level of confidence that...the customer would feel well treated and served...We view our people as sales professionals. They don't need rules. They need basic guideposts, but not rules. You can do anything you need to at Nordstrom to get the job done, just so long as you live up to our basic values and standards."

JIM NORDSTROM

Richard Branson, chairman of Virgin shares this belief. "All you can do is hire the right people and empower them to sort things out as they happen."

If you have employed the right people and the right leaders, if you have the right metrics and rewards in place, you shouldn't need vast amounts of policies. Nevertheless, whatever policies and procedures you do implement, just like the metrics and rewards, should consistently and constantly reinforce the mission, values and vision of your organisation. Put simply: implement the fewest possible policies and procedures necessary to make it easy for your team to exercise their role well and meet their responsibilities. Avoid bureaucracy at all costs.

CULTURE TRUTH #7

Bureaucracy is merely a sledge hammer used to compensate for incompetence and lack of discipline.

SPACE & ENVIRONMENT

"We don't have a lot of time on this earth! We weren't meant to spend it this way. Human beings were not meant to sit in little cubicles staring at computer screens all day."

PETER GIBBONS, OFFICE SPACE

The Facebook offices still have bare walls and unfinished internal decor. Google has slides, a dinosaur and no one is allowed to be more than 100 metres from food. Red Bull's London office is designed to feel more like a lounge and the reception turns into a bar at night. Zappos, the online shoe retailer, has stuck to office cubicles, but encourages each and every employee to customise their space with decorations, toys and trinkets. Staff at Value, the games developer, all have desks on wheels. These global companies and many more besides, spend hundreds of millions of pounds every year to ensure their work spaces are fun, inspiring and foster productivity.

The work environment of your organisation matters.

If you're booking a holiday would you choose a hotel with bare fluorescent lighting in the room; no windows at all; all the walls and furnishings the same colour – grey? Grey walls, grey bed, grey curtains, grey carpet, black and white TV! Of course you wouldn't, because it wouldn't be a very relaxing and uplifting holiday. The space you are in hugely influences your mood and by extension your actions.

The design of your workspace has a massive impact on your teams' productivity and is a useful daily influence to reinforce the mission, vision and values of your organisation. Good spaces that are well-designed can become the means by which your organisation can accelerate achieving goals and reaching the vision.

Facebook's unfinished spaces are a constant reminder to employees that Facebook is always a work in progress. Value's desks on wheels enables employs to move to whatever team they want to work in, consistent with their culture of choice. Zappos daily reinforces their value that the company IS the employees by having them design the spaces. And Google...well who doesn't love a slide and free food!

Researchers have found that effectively designed office environments can inspire creativity and help people to focus their attention. Even the colour of the walls can make a big difference. Test-takers in this research who were surrounded by red walls were better at skills requiring accuracy and attention to detail, while workers in blue environments were more creative. People who worked in high-ceiling rooms were significantly better at seeing the connections between seemingly unrelated subjects. The study references a PhD thesis at the University of Exeter that found enriched work environments improve productivity by around 15%. Not just that, but giving office workers a say in the design upped productivity by 30%.

We've already mentioned the importance of hiring the right people into your organisation and having a well-designed and inspiring work place can help by attracting and keeping the right people. If your spaces reflect who you are (your values) and what you're trying to do (your mission and vision) then the right people will naturally feel at home and want to join you. Daniel Keighron-Foster, CEO of Melbourne, a server hosting company, says "while it may seem a frivolous expense, the idea is to make it impossible for someone to want to leave. If you look at the costs of bringing on a new person, recruitment, months before they're fully productive, the additional cost of the office is easily outweighed."

In the same way you have been deliberate about how you reward and the way you implement procedures, do not leave your spaces to evolve; be deliberate about designing them. Think about how your space reflects your values as an organisation. Decide how you want to use the space to reinforce your mission daily. Find ways to keep the vision of the company permanently in people's consciousness.

Think about what work actually needs to be done in the space. Do people need to collaborate? Do you need to provide spaces where people can be on their own? Do you need space for people just to talk? Kevin Kuske, General Manager of Turnstone Furniture Maker, advises that businesses create zones. "If I want to talk, I stand at the kitchen counter because that's where everyone comes and talks. If I need some privacy, I find two couches pulled together." Similarly, Skype, the internet phone company, nurtures collaboration by having workers sit at benches that allow for an easy exchange of ideas. Yet, headphones are the respected way of signalling "leave me alone, I'm thinking," and the company also offers a variety of small, private places for individuals who need quiet and less stimulation.

Whatever your organisation is trying to achieve, having the right space is vitally important; too important to leave to chance! When you've spent valuable time crafting your mission and defining your systems, don't undermine them with a badly designed space.

Pick a policy - perhaps holidays, maybe working hours, or what about your hiring process? What are the benefits of having a policy? What are the drawbacks (there will be some!)? What does this policy say about how your #organisation thinks? Does it reflect and reinforce your mission, values and vision? Does it need changing? Pick another one...

BATTER UP!

"If not us, then who?
If not now, then when?"

JOHN E. LEWIS

There is it. A simple but extremely difficult to implement framework - The One Framework ™ - for building a thriving successful culture, free from politics and complaining, with massively high performing teams that need little day to day management effort.

1. Deliberately define your One Purpose - your mission, vision, values and strategic anchors.

2. Gather your One Team - people who share the MVV and fit the defined culture.

3. Clarify your One Voice - make sure everything you say and write reinforces your One Purpose.

4. Create your One Focus - be deliberate about your metrics, rewards, spaces and processes to build on your One Purpose.

And across all four of these stages, make sure everything reflects, reinforces and drives the purpose of the organisation. Without this driver, your organisation is in danger of becoming inauthentic and unattractive for both customers and employees.

Get it right and you'll create a place where you love to work; a place that inspires you and your team to be your best, and a business that makes more profit too. Not to mention the fact that doing business well has an amazing impact on the world. In 1970, 76% of the world's poor lived in Asia with only 11% living in Africa. However by 1998, through economic growth, China and India successfully lifted so many people from poverty that those statistics almost reversed with only 15% of the world's poor residing in Asia while 66% were in Africa. Business can have a massive impact on people, nations and regions. Building businesses with authentic cultures built around an inspiring purpose is the way to have that impact.

BUT, profit-at–all-costs is a dangerous aspiration. It is pure and simple greed, and by aiming directly for it, businesses will often lose that which they were chasing.

Theodore Malloch sums it up very well when he writes that though a company's well-being relies on profit:

"...by seeking at all costs to be profitable, we destroy the conditions on which profitability depends. We alienate our workforce or the local community, we destroy incentive and undermine the workplace as a forum for

communal life, we become locked in old and once
profitable ways long after the competition has made
them unprofitable, and so on. The story has been told
many times and in many ways. But the essence is
simple: success in a market economy does not come
because you aim at it; success comes because you
have found your ecological niche and can flourish there
by doing your own valuable thing. And doing your own
thing must have a social, moral and spiritual dimension if
it is to attract the loyalty and commitment of the people
with whom and for whom you do it."

THEODORE MALLOCH

So, go and build businesses with a culture where people
thrive, a culture focused on a greater purpose, a culture
that is consistent and authentic.   Define an inspiring
mission; operate with non-negotiable values; drive
towards a 'big hairy audacious' vision; journey with people
who share your vision and fit your culture; recruit the help
of truly great leaders; reward people according to your
purpose; manage and lead according to your values; live
and behave how you expect others to live and behave.

If you do, your people will be happier and stop
complaining, politics will be gone, productivity will soar,
profits will rise, your life as a leader will become easier and

what's more, my friend, you may just change the world.

Good luck!

CULTURE TRUTHS

CULTURE TRUTH #1

When people come together for a purpose
a shared culture will form.

CULTURE TRUTH #2

For better or worse, your culture will influence every
aspect of your organisation.

CULTURE TRUTH #3

A culture is only truly defined by the way people behave
and not what people say!

CULTURE TRUTH #4

You can train someone for skill, but it's far more difficult
to change someone's heart and passion!

CULTURE TRUTH #5

What you say must match how you behave
to create a truly authentic culture.

CULTURE TRUTH #6

What you measure and the behaviours you praise or
punish will become your culture.

CULTURE TRUTH #7

Bureaucracy is merely a sledge hammer used to compensate for incompetence and lack of discipline.

THE ONE
FRAMEWORK

Wherever two or more people come together for a common purpose a shared culture will arise. It doesn't matter whether you spend time explicitly defining your culture or whether you allow it to develop organically, unspoken over time, every single organisation, community or group of individuals, no matter how small or large, will develop a culture - a common set of social rules and values that influence and define everything within the organisation.

And if culture influences and affects every aspect of your organisation, then why would you leave it to chance? The One Framework ™ is a simple and highly effective way of assessing and defining the culture you actually want.

DEFINE YOUR ONE PURPOSE

Your purpose helps you be clear about exactly what it is your organisation does and why it does it. It's the first step to building and explicit culture.

CREATE YOUR ONE TEAM

Getting the right people on the bus is imperative to being

able to execute your purpose and reach your organisational goals with minimum fuss.

FIND YOUR CONSISTENT ONE VOICE

Everything you say and write contributes to defining and building the true culture of your organisation. Be clear and consistent.

MAKE SURE THERE IS ONE FOCUS

Processes and procedures of an organisation, the way you do things, define and shape the true culture. Do they all pull in the same direction?

ABOUT THE
CULTURE GUY

Ben has a passion to inspire, motivate, excite and challenge organisations to be brilliant. He wants to encourage business to be built on a foundation of inspiring mission, honest core values and an audacious vision.

Ben Drury is an entrepreneur, a very experienced coder and trained social worker. He understands people and cultures and is a dynamic, entertaining and innovative speaker, who has honed his skills during 15 years involvement in stage productions. He has worked touring with theatre companies, designing internet banks, writing and directing stage productions, developing and delivering leadership training courses, managing small businesses, building web applications and developing social media strategies.

He now lives in South East London with his wife and three children, coaching, writing, speaking, coding, and watching NFL!

PHOTOGRAPHS

- Open Tin before 'Contents'
  Mathias Kolban – taken from www.pixabay.com

- Champagne before 'Acknowledgements'
  Dariusz Sankowski – taken from www.pixabay.com

- Running track before 'Come on in the water's great'
  Marvin Ronsdorf - taken from www.unsplash.com

- Yoghurt before 'It's not just for yogurt'
  Soorelis – taken from www.pixabay.com

- Lighthouse before 'What do you do all day?'
  Joshua Hibbert – taken from www.unsplash.com

- Boss Mug before 'Who's in who's out?'
  Brooke Lark – taken from www.unsplash.com

- Shouting before 'What's that you say?'
  Jason Rosewell – taken from www.unsplash.com

- Lens before 'What happened in here?'
  John Allen – taken from www.unsplash.com

- Baseball before 'Batter Up!'
  Pets! – taken from www.unsplash.com

- Ben Drury before 'About the culture guy'
  Stephanie Lumsden – donated by the photographer.

38867128R00107

Printed in Poland
by Amazon Fulfillment
Poland Sp. z o.o., Wrocław